Washington, DC

WASHINGTON, DC

Photography provided by Richard Berenholtz, Buff Black, Carol Diehl, Carol Highsmith, Dai Hirota, David Frazier/DanitaDelimont.com, Steve Rokbury/DanitaDelmimont.com, Dianne Dietrich Leis, Everett C Johnson, Henryk T. Kaiser/Transparencies, Inc., James Blank, James Lemass, Jon Ortner, National Parks Services, Padro Images, Pat & Chuck Blackley, Peter Gridley, Richard Nowitz/Photri-Microstock, Photri-Microstock, Russ Finley, Scott T. Smith, Scott T. Smith/DanitaDelimont.com, Steve Alterman and Werener Bertsch/Bruce Coleman Inc.

ISBN-13 978-1-60068-247-6

Second Printing, December 2008

4961 Windplay Drive, El Dorado Hills, CA 95762
www.impactphotographics.com

Printed in China

The Thomas Jefferson Memorial stands as a symbol and a reminder of the things that Jefferson wanted for this country: equality, education, liberty, freedom, and independence.

The Capitol of the United States crowns Capitol Hill in Washington, DC. It houses the legislative branch of government, which is comprised of the House of Representatives and the Senate.

From the top of the Washington Monument, each visitor is treated to an unequaled view of the city of Washington. Visibility can be over 40 miles on a clear day from the tallest structure in the city.

Architect Henry Bacon designed the Lincoln Memorial in the style of the Doric temples of ancient Greece.

Surrounded by 36 columns, symbolizing the number of states in the Union at the time of Lincoln's death, the memorial houses the sculpture of Lincoln by Daniel Chester French.

The red sandstone Smithsonian Institution building, with its light crenellated towers, symbolizes the entire institution to many visitors. Popularly known as the "Castle," this building housed all the Smithsonian's operations when it opened in 1855. Today, it houses the Smithsonian Information Center.

The National Mall, a tree-lined, grassy space, was part of Pierre L'Enfant's 1791 plan for the city of Washington. Today it stretches from the Capitol to the Lincoln Memorial and is lined on either side with buildings of the Smithsonian Institution.

The White House has been the home of every president of the United States since John Adams. It is significant for its Federal architecture, as a symbol of the presidency, and for the important decisions made within its walls over the years.

The Thomas Jefferson statue is situated inside the Memorial facing toward the White House. It was designed to represent the Age of Enlightenment and Jefferson as a philosopher and statesman. The bronze statue is 19 feet tall and weighs five tons.

The United States Capitol crowns Capitol Hill and commands the attention as the symbolic center of Washington, DC.

This temple of liberty memorializes the ideas and ideals of the American Revolution while providing the forum for debates, deliberations, and decisions by the people's elected representatives.

Arlington Cemetery provides a quiet resting place for many of the nation's honored dead. Row upon row of white stones mark the graves of soldiers who gave their lives for the country.

Descending into the earth before rising again, the Vietnam Veterans Memorial Wall bears the names of the more than 58,000 Americans who died or remain missing in the Vietnam War.

The Washington Monument was built in honor of George Washington. It is shaped like an Egyptian obelisk and is 555 5/8 feet high. It was finished on December 6, 1884.

The U.S. Marine Corps War Memorial stands as a symbol of this grateful nation's esteem for the honored dead of the U.S. Marine Corps. While the statue depicts one of the famous incidents of World War II, the memorial is dedicated to all Marines who have given their lives in the defense of the United States since 1775.

The Supreme Court Building, completed in 1935, was designed in the classical Corinthian architectural style to complement nearby congressional buildings. The Supreme Court Justices are nominated by the President and confirmed with the advice and consent of the Senate.

The Smithsonian National Museum of the American Indian is the first national museum dedicated to the preservation and study of the Native American way of life.

The United States Capitol is among the architecturally impressive and symbolically important buildings in the world. It has housed the meeting chambers of the Senate and the House of Representatives for over two centuries.

The Lincoln Memorial is a tribute to President Abraham Lincoln and the nation he fought to preserve during the Civil War (1861-1865). This 19-foot sculpture of a seated Lincoln is in the center of the memorial chamber.

Situated on the south side of the Tidal Basin in West Potomac Park, the Thomas Jefferson Memorial is one of the city's picturesque landmarks.

Dedicated in 1943, on the 200th anniversary of Jefferson's birth, this circular white marble memorial is in keeping with the classical style favored by the third U.S. president, architect, scholar and political thinker.

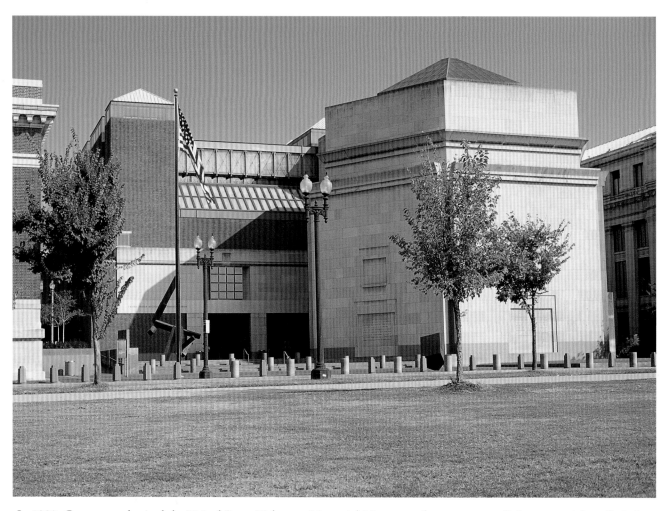

In 1980, Congress authorized the United States Holocaust Memorial Museum to be a permanent living memorial to all victims who perished in the Holocaust. The building has been designed as a living institution dedicated to research and teaching, as well as to contemplation and commemoration.

Commemorating the great principles of democracy, the Lincoln Memorial, Washington Monument, and Capitol align along a line conceived by Pierre L'Enfant in 1791.

The Chesapeake and Ohio Canal National Historical Park preserves America's Canal era and transportation history. Originally, the C&O Canal was a lifeline for communities and businesses along the Potomac River. Today millions of visitors hike or bike the canal, enjoying all of the cultural and recreational opportunities it has to offer.

If the Capitol is the living symbol of the democratic process, the Lincoln Memorial reminds us of the constant vigilance necessary to ensure that social justice and national unity continue for future generations.

The Great Hall in the Jefferson Building of the Library of Congress is a magnificent display of architecture. The ceiling is 75 feet above the marble floor and is decorated with stained glass skylights.

Mount Vernon was the home of George Washington for over 45 years. The house was built in 1743 by George Washington's half brother, Lawrence Washington, who named the property after his commander in the British navy, Admiral Edward Vernon. George Washington acquired the property in 1754 and lived there until his death in 1799.

Inside Ford's Theatre, the State Box, also called the President's Box, has been reconstructed to look as it did on the night of Lincoln's assassination. The furniture and flags in the box were duplicated especially for the restoration, except for the crimson damask sofa and the framed engraving of George Washington, which are originals.

On display in the Rotunda of the Smithsonian National Museum of Natural History is the African Bush Elephant from Angola. At 13.2 feet from the top of its shoulder to its forefoot, it is the largest of its kind on display in the world.

The Pentagon is the headquarters of the United States Department of Defense. It houses approximately 23,000 military and civilian employees. It has five sides and seven floors including two underground and five ring corridors per floor for a total of 17.5 miles of corridors.

As a supporter of cultural arts, President John F. Kennedy took initiative in raising funds to create a National Cultural Center located along the Potomac River. The Kennedy Center opened in 1971 premiering a Requiem Mass composed and conducted by Leonard Bernstein and performed in honor of President Kennedy.

The White House has been the home of every president of the United States since John Adams.

The exterior of the main structure, despite some additions and minor changes, remains much as it was in 1800. The interior has been completely renovated using the historic floor plan.

The Washington National Cathedral's foundation stone was laid on September 29, 1907 in the presence of President Theodore Roosevelt who declared, "Godspeed the work begun this day." Every president of the United States since then has attended services at or visited the Cathedral.

When opened in 1907, Union Station was the largest train station in the world. It was approximately 200 acres with 75 miles of track. If the Washington Monument were placed on its side, it would fit within the station's concourse.

In his early designs for the Nation's Capital, Pierre L'Enfant laid out a great open space where the nation's public events could be celebrated. Annually, the Fourth of July fireworks commemorate America's independence in the shadow of the Lincoln Memorial and the U.S. Capitol.

THEY (WHO) SEEK TO ESTABLISH
SYSTEMS OF GOVERNMENT BASED ON
THE REGIMENTATION OF ALL HUMAN
BEINGS BY A HANDFUL OF INDIVIDUAL
RULERS... CALL THIS A NEW ORDER.
IT IS NOT NEW AND IT IS NOT ORDER.

Forward-thinking and fearless, Franklin Delano Roosevelt symbolized America in the 1930s and 1940s. Confined to a wheelchair, he led a nation battered by the Depression to find its own momentum, demonstrating to Americans that the national will was stronger than any adversity and that, together, its citizens could prevail.

The World War II Memorial, located on the National Mall, commemorates the sacrifice and victory of the WWII generation. It creates a distinct, evocative and serene tribute, yet remains respectful and sensitive to its historic surroundings.

Clara Barton National Historic Site in Glen Echo, Maryland was established in 1974 and was the first National Park Service site honoring the accomplishments of an American woman. The home reflects Clara Barton's unique blend of professional and personal life.

Honoring the unnamed dead of America's wars, the Tomb of the Unknown Soldier was first erected in 1931 to remember the soldiers who sacrificed their lives during World War I. The tomb is guarded 24 hours a day by sentinels from the elite U.S. 3rd Infantry.

The World War II Memorial opened to the public on April 29, 2004. The memorial honors the 16 million who served in the armed forces, the more than 400,000 who died, and all those who supported the war on the homefront.

Founded in 1751, Georgetown is a neighborhood located in northwest Washington, DC along the Potomac River. It is home to Georgetown University as well as the embassies of France, Mongolia, Sweden, Thailand and Ukraine.

The Smithsonian's National Zoological Park was established by an Act of Congress in 1889.
The giant panda *(Ailuropoda melanoleuca)* is one of the world's rare mammals. It is found in the wild in remote mountainous regions of central China. The giant panda has distinctive markings on its coat and relies on bamboo for its diet.

The nation's history is entwined with the history of Arlington House. Once the home of George Washington's adopted son and, later, of Robert E. Lee, the estate was occupied by Union soldiers during the Civil War. By the war's end, portions of the estate had been converted into a cemetery.

Starting as a spring in Laytonsville, Maryland, Rock Creek travels 33 miles to the Potomac River, winding its way through the nation's capital and Rock Creek Park, one of the early national parks in America. Visitors come here to make a personal connection with history and nature.

The Korean War Veterans Memorial honors those Americans who served, and those who gave their lives during the Korean War.

The Corinthian columns in the National Building Museum are among the largest in the world measuring 75 feet tall and 8 feet in diameter.

Theodore Roosevelt was a man with vision. His greatest legacy was in conservation. After Roosevelt's death on January 6, 1919, citizens wanted to establish a memorial in his honor. This wooded island is a fitting memorial to the outdoorsman, naturalist, and visionary who was our 26th President.

The National Museum of American History opened in January 1964 as the Museum of History and Technology; it was the sixth of now nineteen Smithsonian buildings on the National Mall. It houses artifacts such as Abraham Lincoln's top hat, Edison's light bulb and the Star-Spangled Banner.

The Washington, DC Metrorail which opened in 1976 consists of five lines, 86 stations and over 106 miles of track. It is the second busiest rapid transit system in the United States behind the New York City Subway.

Since 1952, nearly a million visitors a year have come to the National Archives Building on Constitution Avenue to see our nation's Charters of Freedom – The Declaration of Independence, the Constitution, and the Bill of Rights.

The creation of the Lincoln Memorial, Washington Monument and Capitol during this nation's more than 200 years of history celebrates our commitment to government of and for the people of the United States.

The words of Thomas Jefferson have shaped American ideals. Today, many of these impressive, stirring words adorn the interior walls of the Thomas Jefferson Memorial.

Known as the "Avenue of the Presidents" and as "America's Main Street," Pennsylvania Avenue connects the U.S. Capitol with the White House and embodies Pierre L'Enfant's most important symbolic vista.